Cognitive
Behavioral Therapy

An Alternative Treatment for Greater
Personal Happiness and Contentment

BILL ANDREWS

CONTENTS

INTRODUCTION

It doesn't take a rocket scientist to figure out that the world can sometimes get to be a bit too much. It's easy to stress out. It's easy to feel like you have the weight of the world on your shoulders. This is especially true if you find yourself around very toxic people. They engage in habitual behaviors or they spout negativity consistently.

Regardless, you find yourself living in some sort of toxic emotional and psychological soup. You're just too stressed out, too anxious and on edge. Interestingly enough, however, you're not technically suffering from chemical-based depression or anxiety disorder. If you think about it, this is actually worse than people living with some sort of mental condition like chemical depression.

"Chemical" depression is a type of depression where your brain's biochemical compounds and neurotransmitters are not properly balanced. Your nerve cells aren't communicating in the most optimal way and you find yourself depressed. In those situations, generally speaking, selective serotonin reuptake inhibitors can help you quite a bit.

Of course, this doesn't apply across the board. There are a certain percentage of people who do not respond at all to that type of treatment. However, for a large percentage of people suffering from chemical or clinical depression, antidepressants and other chemical-based pharmaceutical treatments can help.

Unfortunately, depression and anxiety as well as a generalized sense of unhappiness cannot be simply dismissed as a product of biochemical processes in the human brain. There's a lot involved. You may have two people who have the same tendency for depression, but if their environment and their attitudes are different, there's a high chance that they won't suffer the same problem.

Make no mistake whether you are going through a tough time or a loved one, there is an alternative that you can try. One very effective alternative treatment to depression and anxiety is cognitive behavioral therapy.

This is therapy that involves changing how you look at things. It doesn't involve chemical compounds. It doesn't synthetic materials which you ingest. Instead, it involves you taking control over how you actively look at your world, yourself and your place in the world.

A large number of people report great results due to their use of cognitive behavioral therapy. If you're looking for a solution that doesn't involve you taking a pill and you're looking for a longer term solution than antidepressant or anti-anxiety medication. You are reading the right book.

In this book, I'm going to step you through what cognitive behavioral therapy is, how it works, a bit of its background as well as the components that need to be in place for it work for you. I'm also going to cover step by step directions on how to use cognitive behavioral therapy, and what you should look for if you seek this kind of help from a trained professional.

I'm also going to step you through a bit of the scientific literature that supports cognitive behavioral therapy, the different types of this therapy, its components and the key elements for success.

After that, I'm going to give you an overview of the benefits of cognitive behavioral therapy as well as its limitations and criticisms.

Please understand there is no such thing as a perfect therapy or solution for anxiety or depression. There will always be advantages and disadvantages. There will always be room for improvement.

CHAPTER 1:

DEFINING COGNITIVE BEHAVIORAL THERAPY

Cognitive behavioral therapy is not something that you try on yourself. It's just not going to happen. You have to work with a trained therapist or counselor. While you do the heavy lifting as far as your personal beliefs and your responses to the outside world go, you need expert guidance. You need somebody who knows what they're doing and who knows what to instruct you. They must have been around the block a few times so they know what to anticipate.

This is a one common misconception about cognitive behavioral therapy or CBT for short. A lot of people think that if they just read a book on CBT, they would know the ins and outs of this alternative therapy system, and they can pretty much treat themselves.

There's more to recovery through CBT than just buying a book and learning techniques. You have to actually put them to use. This is the difficult part. You have to keep using these techniques no matter how inconvenient they can be. You have to keep practicing them no matter how busy you get.

Given these logistical considerations, it's no surprise that a lot of people think that you need specially trained counselors or psychiatrists to go through a CBT program. Most of the time, the main value these professionals bring to the table is they give you a formal structure for CBT. You can still do it yourself-you just have to give yourself the time, the space, and you need to commit to doing CBT consistently.

It's very hard to get out from under your mental habits if you are trying to do CBT alone. You need to be under the proper guidance of an experienced therapist who not only understands how it works and how its principles can be tweaked to apply your personal situation but who also knows how to measure success.

You have to understand that this is a results-based therapy. You don't just undergo CBT because you're just trying to "feel better". Who knows what that means? It's too subjective.

When you're working with a trained cognitive behavioral therapist, you are made aware of how your interpretations of things happening in your life impact your feelings, your interpretation of reality and, ultimately, your behavior.

The main goal of cognitive behavioral therapy is not just to feel good or feel at peace. Medication can do that. Being with the right people can do that.

Instead, CBT aims for something higher. It seeks to teach you how to effectively interpret life in such a way that you remain positive, empowered and in control. In other words, with the proper guidance, CBT would help you handle your life in a very different way.

People who normally seek cognitive behavioral therapy feel that their life is spiraling out of their control. They feel that they're stuck. It's as if they're watching a movie of their life, and they really can't do anything about it except just sit back and let things happen.

Properly implemented, cognitive behavioral therapy enables you to reclaim your personal power over your life. Believe it or not everything that happens in your life is your responsibility ultimately.

A lot of people try to run away from this truth. In fact, to a lot of people, this is quite inconvenient and uncomfortable.

Unfortunately, regardless of how we feel, the truth is still the truth. We are always in control of how we respond to the world and this response is never neutral. It always has an impact on what we feel and, ultimately, what we do.

Cognitive behavioral therapy focuses on how people make sense of their world in terms of their interpretation. This is the foundation of cognitive behavioral therapy.

When you change the interpretation, you change how people emotionally respond to things, and this can lead to a profound impact on how they do things.

For example, somebody who is suffering from low self-esteem issues usually looks at any situation from a perspective of doubt. They don't think they're good enough. They don't think they're good-looking enough. They don't think people would like them. They don't think they would belong, so on and so forth.

Since this is how they interpret the signals people and situations give them, it is no surprise that they tend to miss out on opportunities or avoid social settings. They doubt themselves so much. They feel that people would not like them. They feel uncomfortable.

This is not just happening in their heads because when somebody has such a low self-esteem, and they're doubting themselves all the time, this can have physical effects .You can physically feel like you're about to throw up. You feel like you're shaking. You want to curl up into a ball or assume the fetal position.

Unfortunately, people with low self-esteem think that this is natural. They've responded to the world this way for so long they think that it's part of them. Some even say it's just who they are. It's port of their personality. No, it's not.

Cognitive behavioral therapy goes to the root of the problem. The root of the problem is not that feel that you're ugly or that you assume that you are going to screw things up the moment you are given any kind of responsibility.

Instead, it goes straight to the issue - your low self-esteem. Why is that? Why do you automatically feel that people are not going to like you? Why do you automatically fear social settings or any kind of opportunity you learn? How are you looking at your situation? Are there any alternative interpretations?

A crucial part of CBT beat is the identification of negative thought patterns. They have to be clear about their thought process.

CBT doesn't assume that there's something wrong with you. Instead, you are first walked through the process of clearly describing how you view yourself, how you interpret reality and how you find yourself in certain situations.

There's no right or wrong answer here. The focus is objective truth. In other words, it's all about accuracy.

The next step is to look at the thought patterns involved and understand that it's just one possible train of thoughts.

For example, if you go into a bar and you see a very attractive member of the opposite sex turn around, look at you and laugh. If you have a low self-esteem, you would automatically assume that person is laughing at you. Are there alternative interpretations?

A CBT therapist will step you through the alternatives and help you process that memory in such a way that it doesn't lead to negative thoughts and, ultimately, negative actions.

Maybe in that memory there was somebody cracking a joke behind you or making some faces. Perhaps that good-looking person was looking at that person behind you. It doesn't have to be you.

As long as the alternative interpretation are supported by facts, the CBT therapist can help you come up with a healthier approach to processing social information so you get out from under your social phobia.

Speaking of phobias, CBT is quite effective in this field. Take the case of an individual with dental phobia. This person is just deathly afraid of visiting the dentist. We're not just talking about root canal here. We're talking about just regular cleaning.

A CBT practitioner would ask this person about their past experience going to the dentist. The patient would then go through story after story until they get to the traumatic incident that led to an unhealthy association of the dentist with pain. It may have happened when the patient was five years old.

The therapist would then work with the patient to cut that mental connection between dentist and pain. In other words, they help the person realize that what happened in the past can stay in the past. Just because they had a traumatic experience that one time doesn't necessarily mean that all people going to dentists always suffer the same experience. They may just have been unlucky that day.

Oftentimes, the further we are from the memory, the more we blow it out of proportion. We exaggerate. It may turn out that when the patient was a kid, they just experienced slight pain, but as they got older, they remember the pain as something far worse.

An expert cognitive behavioral therapist can help patients go through this process successfully.

CHAPTER 2:

THE HISTORY OF COGNITIVE BEHAVIORAL THERAPY

CBT was formulated about forty years ago to help treat people suffering from depression. As the years went by, a lot of the techniques and steps developed in CBT to handle depression have been applied to a larger set of mental and emotional disorders.

Starting with depression, CBT has gone on to treat borderline personality disorder, bipolar disorder, anger issues, alcohol and drug abuse, childhood depression, spousal or marital conflict, insomnia, eating disorders, fear of the dentist, all sorts of social phobias as well as generalized anxiety. That is a long list, and it's easy to see why cognitive behavioral therapy has expanded quite a bit because there is a tremendous amount of science as well as success stories behind it.

The world of psychology and psychiatry has actually developed on two tracks. There's always been a "talk therapy" component to treating mental, emotional and personality disorders. However, fairly recently, more and more practitioners have been leaning on hardwired or biological treatments involving a range of chemical compounds.

This really all became really popular when the popular antidepressant Prozac entered the global mental health scene. At that point, a lot of people were thinking that depression is just another illness, kind of like the flu. When you have a head cold, you take a pill. When you're depressed, you take a pill.

This has led to a massive explosion in prescriptions for anti-anxiety anti-depression medication. In fact, if you were to study the top ten most-prescribed medications in the United States, antidepressants and anti-anxiety medication will always make the list.

This has raised a lot of alarms because of the fact that these chemicals do have a tremendous impact on the patients' brain chemistry. Without proper supervision and prolonged use, they can have long-term effects on patient's mental functions.

This is why there's been a renewed and intensified interest in more natural approaches to personality, emotional and psychological issues. Cognitive behavioral therapy can work with antidepressant, anti-anxiety and other medications.

However, patients would be better off if they use a completely chemical-free approach. The person often credited as the pioneer of cognitive behavioral therapy is Dr. Aaron T. Beck. Dr. Beck focused most of his research on the study of depression.

In particular, he wanted to see the connection between depression and the cognition or the ability of depressed people to perceive their reality. He noticed that there was quite a bit of a link between depression and people's cognitive thinking.

Prior to Dr. Beck, the common idea was that depression happens and it leads to negative thinking. Dr. Beck reversed the process. He said that if the cognitive state of the individual patient is positive, then depression can be overcome. It can go the other way instead of simply assuming that if a person is depressed, then it leads to negative thinking, and there's really not much people can do about it.

This was a breakthrough because it led to the core premise of cognitive behavioral therapy which involves taking control of how you think. It may seem like your depressed mental state is automatic. It may seem like you really don't have much control over it, but by taking control over your ability to interpret what things mean in your life, this can lead to you arresting that negative emotional slide to sadness, melancholy and, ultimately, depression.

Dr. Erin T. Beck's pioneering work laid the foundation for cognitive behavioral therapy which has then grown by leaps and bounds and is now applied to a lot of dysfunctions and disorders.

CHAPTER 3:

WHAT ARE THE MAIN COMPONENTS NEEDED FOR COGNITIVE BEHAVIORAL THERAPY SUCCESS?

Make no mistake CBT is a viable treatment option for a wide range of psychological, emotional and coping dysfunctions or disorders.

With that said, different therapies have their own requirements. You need to have the right components for any specific type of therapy to work for you.

In the case of CBT, you need trust between the therapist and the patient. This is non-negotiable. Trust is essential to treatment success in CBT.

On the therapist's or counselor's end, that person must be willing to listen to the patient and follow the patient's progress very closely. This requires a deep level of concern for the patient's welfare and a degree of passion for helping others.

Successful CBT therapists must have a strong sense of empathy. They must be open to the specific information shared by their patient. This way, they can configure or adapt the CBT therapy based on the specific set of personal circumstances of the person they're trying to help.

The patient, on the other hand, must be open, sincere and willing to change. This is crucial. If a patient doesn't believe that he or she has any serious problems, it's going to be very hard for CBT to produce positive results. In many cases, it just doesn't happen.

Think of it this way. If you think you don't have a drinking problem, then you probably would not seek the help of an alcohol abuse counselor. Even if you do go, you might not think that the information that person shares with you is going to do you any good. You're not very likely to take up their advice and produce positive change in your life.

Trust, sincerity and willingness to change are crucial to cognitive behavioral therapy's success.

Please understand that even if you are working with the very best CBT therapist, if you're not willing to put in the work and the attention to the change that you're trying to produce, it's not going to work out for you.

You have to understand that at its core, cognitive behavioral therapy simply means working with somebody so you can help yourself. That's really the bottom line because, at the end of the day, it is you who has to change how you look at certain situations, how you read your interactions with people and how you choose to respond.

All of these are controlled by you. Other people can tell you what to do. They can spell out why responding a certain way would produce better results for you but, at the end of the line, you have to make the call. You have to take action. They can't do it for you.

OTHER FACTORS FOR SUCCESS

On top of the patient therapist dynamic, there are other factors involved like the intensity of the sessions. This is very important because when the therapist covers very sensitive territory and the patient intensively studies and focuses on the therapist's guidelines, this can lead to quite a bit of a breakthrough. It also helps if the sessions are not too spaced apart.

Any kind of information being discovered and shared in the sessions must be clear in the mind of the patient. It must be top of mind for that person to learn from that insight and, most importantly, apply it.

If too much time passes between sessions, the patient might forget the important lessons.

It also helps if the delivery of key important concepts is done in a way that appeals to the person being helped. All of us have what their own learning styles.

Some people are very big on ideas. If you're that type of person, you tend to do well in a classroom setting.

Others are more experiential. We'd like to see things as they play out in front of us. This way, we can see the patterns and connect the dots, and this increases the chances that we will put that information into practice.

Others tend to be more social. They'd like to see these concepts play out in a social setting so they can identify them clearly and put them into practice.

These additional factors have a big impact on how individual thinking patterns are structured. It also has a big effect on retraining people as far as their social skills go.

Finally, these factors come into play with CBT sessions that involve problem solving and activating behaviors.

THE BOTTOM LINE: EVERYBODY IS DIFFERENT

I wish I could tell you that you only need to focus on certain factors and you will be okay. Unfortunately, there is no one-size-fits-all or cookie-cutter solution that works for everybody in all circumstances.

Instead, you have to understand these different components. They're like pieces of the puzzle.

Maybe you would perform better if the treatment sessions were more intense. Perhaps you would do better if the therapist puts you in the right setting. It could also be true that you would respond well if the lessons were spaced very closely together.

The problem with all this is there's only one way to find out. You basically have to go through the therapy and see what you and your therapist can change to produce better results.

Right now, before you start going to sessions, all these factors may seem equally important. However, as you try to discover certain things about yourself, how you think and how you learn CBT techniques, you will see certain patterns. You will be able to connect the dots and come up with something that works best for you.

The bottom line is you will only know once you go through it. There's a lot of trial and error here in terms of what would work best for your situation.

What's important to keep in mind is that just because it doesn't seem to work out in the beginning, it doesn't mean that you have to stop. All that means is that you have to trust your therapist fully so you and that person can come up with a solution that works best for you.

EVERYBODY LEARNS IN DIFFERENT WAYS. NO TWO BRAINS ARE LIKE.

You just have to trust your therapist and foster an open line of communication so you can both learn from each other and your therapist can help you realize the right information at the right time to produce the right outcomes.

CHAPTER 4:

HOW COGNITIVE BEHAVIORAL THERAPY WORKS

Cognitive behavioral therapy does not rely on chemicals to change people's behavior. Instead, it focuses on how people view certain memories and certain personal perceptions that they consider the truth.

It may seem pretty basic. In fact, to some people, it may seem like it doesn't really get to the heart of the matter, as far as phobias, depression, anxiety, and other negative emotional and mental states go.

Upon further investigation, it actually goes quite deep. The essence of cognitive behavioral therapy revolves around the fact that the world's stimuli are essentially neutral. Now, this is going to surprise a lot of people.

A lot of people would think that a building that's on fire has to be a disaster. In their minds, there's really no other way to interpret that. Can you imagine a building on fire with orange and yellow bright flames coming out of it, people screaming, commotion, and smoke everywhere?

It's very easy to conclude that there is really a way to look at this situation. What if I told you that two people looking at that same scene can choose to interpret it in two different ways?

One person might think that it's the end of the world. They hear the screams. They fell the heat and they are just paralyzed.

They're petrified. They don't know what to do.

Other they run around like a chicken with its head cut off, or they just stare dumbfounded by the tragedy unfolding before their eyes. A lot of people respond this way.

What if I told you that there's another approach? For a great number of people, when they see that same collection of stimuli, they calmly get out of the building, walk to an open space, reach into their bag or into their coat pocket, and whip out a mobile phone.

They calmly call the fire department, as well as the local hospital. They understand that people could lose their lives. They understand what's at stake. They do all of these in a very calm, focused and deliberate way.

Now, let me ask you. Which approach produced better results? Do you think you're helping yourself and those around you if you choose to look at the situation like it's some sort of disaster or Armageddon scenario.

Unfortunately, you're not doing anybody any big favors. If you think that it is the end of the world, you become emotionally paralyzed. You overload yourself with emotions. You aren't good for much of anything. You just freeze up.

Now, on the other hand, if you look at the exact same facts and conclude that this is solvable and that there is a way out of this situation, chances are there will be more people living through that disaster.

There is no dispute as to what happened. The building still went up on flames. People are still homeless. Some people are in danger of burning. The big issue is how to interpret the same set of facts.

The facts are not going to change. What changes is how we choose to respond. This is the core of cognitive behavioral therapy.

You may have had a situation in your life where somebody touched you in a sexual way. This is somebody you trusted. This is somebody who is very close to you. You felt betrayed back then. You felt let that.

It's as if your world fell apart because this person who you respected, loved, and adored betrayed your trust. Nobody's going to dispute that this actually happened.

The problem is how you're going to choose to interpret that. Are you going to interpret these facts that it continues to hold you back and drag you down from the life fulfilment and peace that you deserve, or are you going to take an alternative path?

Nobody's saying that those facts did not happen. Nobody's saying that you should just forget about those facts because they don't matter. What's important is how you choose to respond in the here and now.

Is your response going to help you lead a more balanced and effectively life? Alternatively, are you going to keep dragging back all these painful memories and making them worse today by possibly exaggerating them, reading in all sorts of frustrations into them, or otherwise playing a trick on yourself.

Unfortunately, a vast majority of people do not understand that they have this power. They do not realize that they have the ability to look at the world in such a way that they don't have to feel sad, let down, depressed, or anxious.

They don't have to be addicts. They don't have to have all sorts of negative personality and emotional or psychological disorders. A lot of those are actually coping mechanisms.

THE CORE OF COGNITIVE BEHAVIORAL THERAPY

Since CBT focuses on changing how you interpret stimuli, it's crucially important that you be clear on how you think. When a person who needs help doesn't think that their thoughts are negative, then it's going to be very hard to help that person.

If they don't think that how they interpret life's stimuli holds them back, it's going to be all that more difficult to get that person's life to change. The core of cognitive behavioral therapy is simple clarity.

Are you clear that these thoughts are negative? Are you clear about the fact that when you think these thoughts and interpret them a certain way, you end up saying the wrong things, feeling the wrong emotions, and doing the wrong actions?

Are you aware that this leads to some sort of vicious cycle or a downward spiral? Let's say you have negative memories in the past.

If you interpret them in such a negative way that you say negative things today, people of course, will respond in such a way that you can easily interpret as negative. You then feel bad and you react in a negative way some more.

It becomes a self-fulfilling prophecy. Who told you that you're ugly? Who told you that you're worthless? Who told you that you're a loser?

Those are interpretations. Clarity is crucial. For a lot of people, clarity also requires trust. You have to trust yourself that you make the right decisions.

Unfortunately, a lot of us have lost trust in ourselves. We feel that our lives are spiralling out of control and there's really not much we can do. Everything is in the hands of other people. We are rocked backwards and forwards by situations outside of our control.

Well, these are just interpretations. We have chosen them. We have control over them. We can take ownership of them if we want to.

The CBT therapist's job is to first get the patient to clearly assess how they think. We're not even going to say that it's negative, positive, or less than optimum. We're not even going to apply any labels to what's going on.

Instead, the therapist just wants the patient to sit down and have a clear understanding of what is going on. What are they thinking about? What kind of facts come to mind? How do they interpret those facts and what is produced by that interpretation?

They are asked to honestly and accurately say what happens when they think about something, how they feel when they say something, and what they often do when they're feeling certain emotions. The most important aspect of this is the sense of ownership the patient gets.

This thoughts don't come out of nowhere. They're your thoughts.

Nobody put them in your brain. Nobody's pointing a gun at your head, demanding that you think those thoughts.

This is the first step— clarity, from which a sense of ownership or control flows. Once the therapist is able to get the patient to admit that this is how they think, they are then in the position to take ownership of how they think.

The next step is to understand that there are two sides of every story. In the first step, we have a clear understanding of what we're thinking about and how we feel about those things. We also have a clear realization of how we interpret facts.

The next step is to look at those facts and see if there are alternative interpretations. For example, you're looking for a job and you send out a hundred resumes, only to get a hundred rejections.

You're thinking to yourself, "I am unemployable. I am a total and complete failure. I'm a loser." Now, please understand that the facts are the same. The fact is you sent out a hundred resumes. The fact is none of those resumes led to a job interview.

Here's the question that the CBT therapist will ask. Given these facts, is the judgement or the conclusion that you are a loser or somehow unemployable the only logical conclusion?

Could it be that you sent out your resume at the end of November and December, where there is a steep drop in employment? Could it be that you're targeting jobs in a particular industry that is seasonal or it is on a downturn?

Could it be that you did no write your resume well enough? Maybe you left out some important details. Maybe you did not have the time to polish your resume. Could it be that you needed a cover letter, instead of just sending out a resume?

When the therapist talks about alternatives this way, you as the patient are forced to look at the facts that you thought were so black and white in a different way. You start getting that, "Aha!" moment.

You start thinking, "Oh okay. I was instantly jumping to the worst conclusion. I was instantly thinking of the worst case scenario." CBT teaches you to become fully aware of your thought process and your conclusions from them.

It doesn't grab you by the neck and say to you, "You're thinking the wrong way. You're thinking negative thoughts or you're thinking about things that you shouldn't be thinking about."

It doesn't do that. Instead, it just puts you in a position to take ownership of what is going on after you are clear about the judgements that you make.

After you are clear about alternative interpretations to the facts of your life, the therapist would coach you how to interpret the same set of facts in a way that pushes you upward or is at least neutral. The ideal is to swap out negative assessments and replace them with positive ones.

If this isn't the case, then at the very worst, the CBT therapist would want you to come up with a neutral conclusion. Another approach would be for the therapist to challenge the patient to look at the past traumatic experience in a different light. How?

The patient is challenged to look for the things that went right. It's very easy to focus only on the things that went wrong. It doesn't take much effort to concentrate on the things that are missing or the areas for improvement.

It does take quite a bit of effort to look at the big picture and understand that there were many other things that were going right. This creates a sense of perspective.

This enables the patient's attitude to change. They start interpreting the experience not from that narrow lens that just focuses on the perceived failure, shortcoming, harm, insult, embarrassment, humiliation, and the negative emotional states at that point in time.

Instead, the person is invited to look at the big picture by paying attention to the things that went right. Everything then falls into place. It doesn't make the hurt go away nor does it make the facts go away, mind you.

However, the patient gets perspective. This enables them to have a healthier frame of mind when it comes to that past trauma. It may well be that as this person got older, the more they exaggerated things in their mind.

It's not unusual for people to have a fairly minor experience in the past. However, given how frustrating their lives have become, they start looking at this past experience as some sort of reason or excuse for why they're struggling in the present day.

This often takes the form of blowing things out of proportion or exaggerating things in your mind. This is the complete process of cognitive behavioral therapy. It's all about changing how you interpret stimuli, either from past memories or information that you are currently receiving.

WHY IS PERSONAL INTERPRETATION SO IMPORTANT?

When you choose how you interpret the neutral stimuli that the world is throwing your way, you are in more control. You can choose an interpretation that makes you feel more confident and enables you to be more effective.

It doesn't have to be the end of the world. The experience you just had doesn't have to be some sort of personal insult. It doesn't have to dismiss you as a total person.

The way you interpret stimuli impacts your emotional state. Your emotional state in turn, impacts what you choose to do. When you go through this process in an unmindful way, you would think that this is all automatic.

You would think that there's really nothing you can do because the moment you start encountering certain things, instinct kicks in. You just end up saying certain things and taking certain actions.

It doesn't have to be that way. You have control over your emotions, your actions, and most importantly your thoughts. You don't have to interpret this memory the exact same way you've been handling out for all these years.

You can choose to change how you interpret. This is the essence of CBT. It's all about changing the mind-set, which leads to a change in attitude and a change in behavior and speech.

These flow into each other. When you make a positive change in how you interpret things, you start acting in a more positive way. This leads to more positive reactions from people around you.

You then feel happier because you are well-received. People are sending you the right signals. This makes it much easier for you to interpret the world in the best possible light.

This then makes you feel emotionally positive, which leads to you taking more effective action. You're doubting yourself less. You're feeling less anxiety. You suffer less depression.

This can create an upward spiral. This is the foundation of cognitive behavioral therapy. It all boils down to how you interpret reality.

CHAPTER 5:

INTERVENTION STEPS PRACTICED BY COGNITIVE BEHAVIORAL THERAPY COUNSELORS AND PROFESSIONALS

As a counselor, these are the steps you have to follow with your client. We'll take the case of depression because this is the most common. If you have a client who is suffering from depression, follow the steps below.

STEP #1: FIND THE PROBLEM AREA IN YOUR LIFE

When somebody's depressed, it's very easy to just say, "I'm depressed." That blanket statement, unfortunately, doesn't really say much. You're just sharing your emotional state.

It's also a clinical diagnosis. It may turn out that you're just sad. Depression, in medical terms, is tightly defined. There's a lot of things that go into depression.

Usually, people use that word very casually. Regardless, the first step is to find the problem areas in your life. What causes this frustration that leads to depression? Is it your relationship? Is it your job or your business?

Does this have something to do with school or health and fitness? Are you having problems with regret? Maybe you feel you picked the wrong spouse. Maybe you think that you are stuck in the wrong job. Regardless, you need to be clear about what parts of your life make you sad or depress you.

STEP #2: BE CONSCIOUS AND AWARE OF YOUR AUTOMATIC THOUGHTS

This is where the robber meets the road. It's easy to say that you have problem areas in your life. Maybe you're stressed out or depressed about not having any money. That part is easy.

You have to look at what triggers your automatic thoughts. Is it that time of the month when you get a big fat envelope from the credit card company with a huge balance? Does it involve your landlord knocking on your door asking for the month's rent?

Whatever the case may be, zero in on what triggers automatic thoughts of depression or extreme sadness. Look for your triggers. This is not always external.

It doesn't have to take the form of a person. It doesn't have to play out as some sort of situation. It can also be a memory.

It's not unusual for people to feel really angry or anxious when an image flashes in their mind. Maybe it's the image of your father who abandoned you as a kid.

Maybe it's an image of an ex who betrayed you by screwing around behind your back. Maybe it's the image of the school bully that humiliated you on a daily basis.

Perhaps it's the face of your boss who love to hate. Maybe it's a very humiliating experience in the past where a lot of kids ganged up on you, beat you up, or laughed at you.

Whatever the case may be, be conscious of your automatic

thoughts. Don't automatically assume that just because a certain image flashes in your mind, that there's really only one way to respond.

You may even be thinking that this is the only natural way. It isn't. It's all in your head. You think it's natural, but it turns out that it isn't. It may turn out that you are responding in the least optimal way.

STEP #3: ANALYZE YOUR "AUTOMATIC THOUGHTS" AND THEIR IMPACT ON YOUR DECISIONS

The cognitive behavioral therapist will first get the patient to lay out what they think automatically. For example, you went through several bad breakups when you were in high school or in college. These really damaged your self-esteem and your self-confidence. They were quite traumatic.

The therapist would then ask you to describe what happened. He or she would then ask you to describe what you think about these memories now and how they impact the way you think, what you talk about, and what you do.

From that point, the therapist would also ask you how your decisions are impacted by your interpretations of these facts.

Through this process, the patient will be the one to realize that the decisions and actions he or she takes may not be all that rational. They may be blowing things out of proportion, they may have lost all perspective, they may be reading too much into what happened in the past, and this is leading them to constantly make the same wrong decisions over and over again.

What's important to note here is that the therapist is not the one making these conclusions. It is not as if this person would say to your face after you tell them what's going on that you are wrong. That's not their job. Their job is to facilitate your self-discovery process so you see the disconnect between how you're judging reality and what you base that judgment on.

You yourself will see the disconnect. You yourself will see that you're drawing all these irrational conclusions from facts. These facts are not going to go away.

Yes, somebody broke your heart. Yes, you got sexually abused. Yes, you got beaten down and physically abused. Those are not going to go away. Facts are facts.

What can go away is the irrational decision or, at the very least, the decisions that you make that are not all that optimal. These decisions continue to hurt you again and again in the here and now.

STEP #4: RECOGNIZE NEGATIVE PATTERNS AND ACTIVELY DISTANCE YOURSELF FROM THEM

The first step to change is not to destroy all negative links. That's too much to ask for. Instead, now that you know where your negative decisions and emotional states are coming from, you need to pay attention to what triggers them.

Pay attention to the almost automatic process of you perceiving something or remembering something, and then feeling negatively. And just as quickly, doing something negative. It's as if you are trying to stop a roller coaster or a runaway train. I'm sure you know that that's almost impossible.

The good news is, by simply being aware of all these connections, you start getting perspective. You start realizing that you don't have to go through the same process that you have habitually gone through. This is the same process that made you feel really lousy at the end.

It doesn't have to end up that way. By understanding how all of these are connected and you start labeling this as something negative, you position yourself to eventually walk away from that old chain reaction.

The first step to creating a better reaction is to recognize, and then put yourself in a position to walk away. This can take quite a while. Don't expect any overnight miracles.

You've been thinking negatively for so long. The negative decisions that you have made have impacted your life profoundly. It would be too much to expect that you would break out of this overnight.

But Step 4 is a significant step because it positions you to have the ability to stop thinking negatively. You're not quite there yet, but this is a turning point.

STEP #5: ACTIVELY COMBAT EVERY UNDERLYING ASSUMPTION YOU MAKE

When you engage in "automatic thinking," you're basically allowing yourself to get carried away by your assumptions. You let them get the better of you.

This doesn't have to be the case. This doesn't have to happen, believe it or not.

One way you can take the power out of this automatic chain reaction is to question the assumptions behind what triggers you. For example, you're walking into a class, and this extremely attractive member of the opposite sex starts laughing in your general direction. As you get closer, that person laughs some more.

The negative interpretation of this scene is so obvious that it doesn't need explanation. You're probably interpreting this in a very negative way. Your assumption is that that person is laughing at you.

Question that assumption. Are there facts that would support that that person is not laughing at you? Pay attention to what's happening in the scene.

Do you remember it clearly? Is somebody whispering to that person's ear and then pointing to himself or herself and making some sort of gesture? It may well be that that person is joking with the person laughing. It can turn out that that person is making a joke of herself or himself.

Believe it or not, that scene that you keep playing in your mind of that personal insult, humiliation and embarrassment might not be all about you. In fact, it might not have anything to do with you. It might have everything to do with the inside joke those two people were sharing.

Question your assumptions because if you don't, this would be invisible. Those details would not exist in your mind. All you see is the person laughing at you. All you can dwell on is your sense of embarrassment and humiliation.

Think of it like a movie scene. You see that person laughing. There's a lot of other people around that person, there's all sorts of commotion, and then there's you walking through the scene.

If you think that that person's actions are all about you, and this was some sort of personal insult, what do you do? Well, you basically crop out the rest of the scene. It's as if everything turns black and white and fades into the background, and the only thing that is in live, vivid color is the person laughing.

That is not a realistic movie. There are many other details out there. Believe it or not, these details provide context, and this context might not lead to the conclusion that you automatically jump to.

Do not be afraid to question your assumptions. Allow yourself to be wrong. Allow yourself to believe that there are alternative explanations. Otherwise, you're going to get hit by that freight train of emotions. It just hits you at full speed and power because you assumed too much.

You might want to knock out its power by looking at your assumptions. It may well turn out that things are not what you think they are. At the very least, you put yourself in a position to interpret the scene in such a way that you are emotionally neutral.

Forget about a positive interpretation. Let's assume that that's not possible. At least shoot for something neutral. You don't have to constantly beat yourself up.

STEP #6: TRY TO SEE THINGS FROM A POSITIVE PERSPECTIVE

Perspective is an art form. It's not a science. Different people can come up with different perspectives. That's just the way it is.

Some people have an instinct or a knack for gaining perspective. They just zoom out and they see the big picture. They see the different pieces of the puzzle.

Other people cannot do that. They dwell on one particular detail and allow it to eat away at them.

Chances are, if you're reading this book, you are more like the latter instead of the former. That's okay. There's no right or wrong answer. What's important is you understand the power of positive perspective and you actively work towards it.

I don't care if you are automatically a negative person, I don't care how long you've been thinking negatively, you have it in you to gain this positive perspective. You just have to claim it. You just have to practice it day after day after day. It takes work.

It's kind of like going to the gym. Remember the first time you hit the weights at the gym? It was murder. No other word would do the experience justice. I mean, your muscles were very flabby and weak and even flat.

When you started lifting weights, you put a lot of pressure on your muscles, and they hurt. But the secret is, when your muscles get sore, that's precisely when you decide to keep going to the gym.

Because your muscles have a memory. And if they absorb all that constant pressure, they quickly tighten. You quickly move out of the soreness phase and your muscles start to fall into place. That's how it works. Don't let the pain throw you off.

The same goes with trying to see events and situations from a positive perspective. There are many different perspectives out there, you're just going to have to identify the positive ones and continue to hammer on them until they become part of your consciousness.

You have to continue picking these until these become your default standard. It is not easy, but it can be done. Just as it isn't easy to go to the gym day after day, even if your body is aching, it can be done. And you would be richly rewarded for it.

STEP #7: DESTROY THE POWER OF THE WORST-CASE SCENARIO

Now that you have the ability to look at things in a more positive perspective, the next step is to understand that the reason why you feel so negatively or you get thrown off is because you always assume the worst-case scenario.

For example, you go to a job interview and the recruiter looks at your resume and then looks at you and gives you a weird look. You can interpret this as essentially signaling that you are unemployable.

You're more than welcome to interpret this as a sign of failure; that you're some sort of unemployable loser. What is the worst-case scenario? That employer will not hire you. So what?

Ask yourself that question. So what? What happens next?

Well, you know what happens next. You go down the list.

There's another employer out there. There are tons of online job sites. There are government jobs. There are jobs in your neighborhood, and other options.

The problem with the worst-case scenario is that it forces you to look at what you're going through as some sort of ultimate disaster. You get into this mindset that there's nothing beyond what's going on in front of you.

But think about it, what is the worst thing that can happen? Your partner leaves you, you get sick, you get fat, you can't get the job or the promotion, you get fired, now what?

When you ask yourself these two questions, you start seeing perspective. You start robbing the worst-case scenario of its tremendous power. These questions, of course, are "Now what?" and "So what?"

Keep asking yourself these questions when you notice that you're entering a negative frame of mind.

When you have identified your assumptions, keep asking these questions. Use them as some sort of battering ram against the deep-seated beliefs that you have about yourself, your competence, your value as a person, and other important beliefs.

You have to understand that these things are only as powerful as you imagine them to be. They draw their power from you.

If you refuse to give them power by constantly asking "So what" and "Now what," you start seeing that there's another world out there. Another world that you can take action on. All is not lost, believe it or not.

STEP #8: WORK BASED ON FACTS

Let's get one thing clear, changing how you think about things takes a lot of work. We also have a lot of fantasies and hopes and wishes regarding our lives.

It's not unusual for people to work based on hopes and wishes and dreams. Some get quite far.

Unfortunately, for most people, this doesn't work. They get stuck in some sort of holding pattern. It's as if they're chasing their tail.

The reason for this is that they're not looking to rebuild their lives and transcend their present realities using facts. This is the key. Base your personal change on reality.

As I mentioned above, facts are facts. You got abused, you got fired unjustly, people slandered you, people hurt you for no good reason, and so and so forth. The list is endless. Now what? So what?

Look at the facts. Are they a complete and total disaster?

For example, your partner left you after several years together, does this mean that it's the end of the world? When you look at the mirror do you see somebody who is just completely unacceptable and so repugnant that nobody in their right mind would want to spend time with you or find value in you?

Of course, not. Look at that fact. That you're still alive, that you can still give, that you can still share. There are just so many things out there. And if you're honest enough, you have a long list of the things that you can offer.

These are facts. They're not going to go away. They're just as solid as the facts of the negative experience or your negative situation. These are the foundation or building blocks of a new perspective.

This is why people who are able to achieve long lasting change in their lives continue to persist because they built the change on facts. They don't build a new life based on what they hope to be true or they assume to be true. That's not going to work.

That's like trying to build a huge structure on sand. It only takes one storm to destroy that building. It's built on sand. Are you building your new life on the sand of wishes and hopes and dreams?

Focus on the facts. Do you have a job? Do you have skills? Can you speak well enough?

These are the types of questions you should ask yourself if you keep coming up with the conclusion that you're unemployable, you'll never ever make money, and other toxic beliefs that hold you back and drag you down from living up to your fullest potential.

Focus on the facts that you have. The fact that you're alive is a big deal. The fact that both your kidneys are working and your lungs are in good shape, those are big deals.

Build your new assumptions and your new perspective on facts. This way, you're realistic. You're not trying to bend reality and insert stuff that doesn't really exist because it's not sustainable.

You're definitely welcome to try, and I'm sure you can achieve some results, but if you really are looking for something sustainable that would withstand the test of time, build on reality.

Build on facts.

STEP #9: TAKE OWNERSHIP OF YOUR PERCEPTIONS

In this step, you are going to sum up all the other steps listed above.

In the previous steps, we were just basically isolating the interconnection between facts as they truly exist and your interpretations of them. You are now also fully aware of the impact your interpretations have on the things you think about, how you feel, and your behavior. Now, we're going to take things to a whole other level.

At this point, you know that all these processes are going on. You know, at this point, that your assumptions play a big role in the outcomes you get. At this stage, you're going to take ownership of the whole process. You're going to choose which reality you want for yourself.

This is where judgment comes in. You're going to consciously say, "I know that when I think this way, this is usually what happens. I feel defeated, small, powerless, ugly and hopeless. I know that when I think certain things, it always puts me on that path. This has happened many, many times before."

At this point, your cognitive behavioral therapist would then say, "Do you find other paths?" This is where you start piecing together an alternative.

Please note that you hope that there is a better path. There is an element of wishing here as well.

You obviously wish that there is a better way. You obviously wish for better outcomes. That is obvious. You're not being unrealistic when you do that because that's part of the human condition.

Everybody is drawn to pleasure and tend to shy away from pain. No surprises there. But at this point, your therapist would then work with you to come up with that alternative path.

And by "work with you," I'm not talking about feeding models or plans into your head. They're not doing it right if that's what they're doing. Instead, they prompt you and even challenge you to come up with an alternative.

You know that the way you've always done things leads to negative places. That's a non-starter. So now you're starting over again. Your therapist is then asking you, "What is the better way?"

Come up with a plan. Piece it together. What kind of action steps will you have when certain situations occur?

Maybe it's a past memory, maybe it's a current experience, and maybe it's a predictable pattern that you constantly encounter at work or in some sort of social place. Whatever the case may be, you have to now start coming up with an alternative. This has to be detailed.

You're basically saying to yourself, "Okay, if I say these things one, two and three, I will do x, y and z. I will not do A, B and C. I've been doing A, B and C since forever. Look at me, I'm not happy. I'm not living up to my fullest potential."

You're going to engage in these emotional internal dialogues. It has to be emotional. It has to register at the heart level, otherwise, it's not real.

STEP #10: APPROACH YOUR PERSONAL CHANGE WITH A SENSE OF URGENCY

I've got some bad news for you. I really do. All the information that I've shared here with you is not going to change your life if you do this one thing: keep it in your head.

If you approach the materials that I'm sharing with you from a purely intellectual level, forget about it. Change is not going to happen.

I know that sounds harsh, it might even seem dismissive, but it's true. If you were to look at all the information that I shared with you here and you just file it into your mental cabinets, nothing is going to happen.

You can see the connection, you can see the necessity, you can see the internal logic, you can see patterns, but none of that is going to help you.

It may make all the sense in the world, you may fully understand how cognitive behavioral therapy works, you might have a greater appreciation of the role of the CBT therapist, but your life will continue to remain unchanged.

Why? You did not let it sink into your heart. You did not allow this intellectual information to become emotional information.

People are emotional creatures. We talk a big game about how logical and rational we are. But at the end of the day, we make all sorts of impulsive decisions based on our emotional side.

When we are called out regarding those decisions, that's when our rational side kicks in and we come up with all sorts of seemingly logical explanations for why we made the decisions that we did.

According to a fairly recent psychological research study, consumers were asked regarding their decisions, and it turns out the vast majority actually made the decisions impulsively. But when asked to explain their decisions, they would come up with all sorts of logical or seemingly reasonable explanations.

You have to eventually operate at an emotional level. You have to develop that sense of urgency. Unfortunately, that's not going to happen if you don't let the information that I've shared with you sink to the level of your heart. That's when you will get the drive and the power to keep pushing.

Please understand that what you're doing is very difficult. It really is. It's really hard to change.

We get accustomed to the way we're doing things. Our brains are always looking for the path of least resistance.

Our brains are very powerful and efficient biochemical machines. Once it creates a connection, it's very hard to break that connection. But that's precisely what you need to do.

To get the power to do that consistently over an extended period of time, you need an emotional sense of urgency. This is when you make the transition from viewing cognitive behavioral therapy as a nice little option that you can take if you have the time to something that you must do. This is something that just has to happen, otherwise, you're going to suffer tremendously.

This is how you should think about CBT in your mind. This is how you should frame it. Nothing less will do.

COGNITIVE BEHAVIORAL THERAPY PROGRESSION

What follows is the progression your CBT therapist will step you through to enable you to take fuller control of your thought process and how you take action based on them.

This doesn't have a timeline. Some people can proceed through this list very quickly. Others will take some time.

Everybody's different. No two brains are alike, so don't worry about zipping through this list.

If you are taking much longer, it doesn't mean that there's something wrong with you. It doesn't mean that you are a weak person. It doesn't mean any of that.

Everybody has a different pace. It's perfectly okay if it takes you a long time from point to point. What's important is that you are able to make that journey.

That is what's crucial. Ultimately, the only thing that really matters is that you are taking action on your need to change.

Again, I don't want to repeat myself here, but I need to do it for emphasis. You can read all the information I shared with you here, but until and unless you take action on them, this information is not going to change your life.

You have to act on them. You can't just plug them in your brain and just kick them around like dull, lifeless, intellectual concepts. That's not going to do you any good. You have to take action.

WHAT FOLLOWS IS THE PROCESS:

START WITH A SINGLE THOUGHT

The first thing that you need to do with cognitive behavioral therapy is to zero in on your thoughts on an item by item basis.

Start with one single thought. Pay close attention to how you verbally describe that thought. Are there any loaded words that you are using? Are there any trigger words that you are using? These are emotional words.

For example, there's a big difference between "request" and "demand." There's a big difference between "will" and "may." This may seem small, but if you spot them in how you speak about your thoughts, you learn a lot about your unstated assumptions.

Keep hammering that single thought about yourself. Are there any hidden assumptions? Is it accurate? Is it valid? Does it reflect reality in terms of facts?

EXPOSE ALL ASSUMPTIONS

Now that you have picked away at a single thought that you have about yourself, lay out all the assumptions that this thought depends on.

Assumptions, of course, can vary from the things that you assume that you are perceiving to how you connect what you think you're seeing or perceiving, with things that happened in the past or what will happen in the future.

Lay these all out. There is no right or wrong answer, right off the top of your head. This is a stream of consciousness exercise. Just lay it all out.

Nobody's going to check your work. Nobody should be looking over your shoulder. This is just you. This is private information.

Just lay it out. Don't hold back. You're not going to be offending anybody. You're not going to be letting anybody down. The only person that you're going to disappoint is yourself if you hold back.

So, lay it out. What are you assuming when you think that single thought about yourself?

QUESTION YOUR BELIEFS

Assumptions are beliefs. These are beliefs about what you think are true or how things should be.

Now, using your superior mental processing firepower, hack away at these beliefs. Are these true? Are they true now? Are they going to be true in the future? How good of a job do they do in explaining the past?

How do these beliefs position you? Do they put you in a good light? Do they give you strength? Do they help you become a more effective person?

What kind of facts do they draw on? Are these facts real or are they also assumptions?

In a way, this exercise is similar to taking a ball of string and unwinding it to see smaller knots inside the ball. You unwind those. You take a belief, and you break it apart, and there are smaller beliefs there. Break those apart until you're left with your assessment of reality.

Now, at this stage, you're going to say to yourself, is this accurate or are there alternative interpretations? If it's accurate, does it hurt me? If it hurts me, are there alternative applications that will at least make the overall effect neutral?

When you do this, you see how your beliefs have been distorted. Maybe you're blowing things out of proportion. Maybe you are not looking at the actual facts.

BE SURE YOUR PERSONAL FACTS ARE REALLY FACTS

I know that the subheading title is kind of confusing. But the truth is, when we look at past events in our lives, we often read into them elements that actually arose from later issues in our lives.

It's like a historian going through a war, rewriting history of a battle that took place in the distant past. In this rewrite, all the hopes, dreams, wishes of that historian's society in the here and now is projected onto the past. So, when students in the future will read that historical narrative of a battle that's supposed to have happened a long, long time ago, it actually speaks to the values and objectives of a later date.

Historians do this all the time. Political commentators do this. Politicians definitely do this. And, believe it or not, people living their individual lives do this when it comes to their personal histories.

Well, doing this obviously serves a very important purpose. It gives you a sense of direction. It gives you a sense of meaning. But the problem is, you have to be aware that you're doing this, and you also have to be aware that, ultimately, it's lying.

Facts are facts. Interpretations are interpretations. Know the difference. Know where to draw the line.

This is why you have to look at the facts that you think exists in your life and break them up. Is this really what happened? Are there gaps? Is the timeline correct or has it been shrunk? Has it been pasted together and fused with stuff that happened later on?

This is especially true when it comes to experiences of abuse.

A lot of clinical psychologists and counselors got into a lot of trouble in the past because they were asking the wrong questions to their patients. These questions were loaded. They were not neutral. They did not lay out a neutral platform for the patient to hash out his or her issues.

Instead, they were loaded questions. There were assumptions in them. And it's no surprise that the patient started filling in the assumptions.

If you want to see a horrific example of this, look up the case of the McMartin Day Care. In that case, government social workers interviewed kids regarding sexual molestation and abuse in a day care center.

The questions they asked essentially coached the kids to give the answers the investigators were looking for. This resulted in a series of indictments of people that ran the day care.

It turns out that the kids were basically trying to please the people interviewing them. So, when the interviewee said, "Did this person touch you?" or "How did this person touch you?" all these horrific details would come out. It turns out that this was all imagined information to fit the questions.

You may be doing the same with yourself. You may be reading in all sorts of issues into past facts. And the more you do this, the more hardwired those facts seem. They seem really immovable because, hey, I believed them for so long.

Well, now is the time to take a sledgehammer and start blasting away at the things that you assume are facts. This doesn't take much effort.

You don't have to have a graduate degree to do this. You just basically have to ask the journalists' six questions: who, what, where, when, why and how.

Here's a pro tip: do not start with why. Focus on everything else first. You will quickly find out that a lot of the facts that you have automatically assumed were true are actually spotty at best.

There might be certain key elements missing, but you still assume that this is the truth. But it's missing a key element, and that key element is actually what would justify you making all these negative conclusions based on these facts.

If you were to plug in those missing parts, these facts may well support a completely different conclusion. This is how you know that your beliefs are distorted. You don't have to put yourself through this process.

UNDERSTAND THE POWER OF MOOD

Please understand that when you're looking at past facts and you're trying to make an analysis or you're trying to judge what happened in the past, they're dependent on how you feel at that given point in time.

A lot of people discount this. They think, "Well, facts are facts. I just need to think about certain things and the explanation and the conclusion pretty much jumps out at me. It doesn't take much effort. It's smooth and it flows just like water."

Fine, you can feel that way. But understand that your mood at that time actually impacts how easy it would be for you to accept that conclusion.

And when you're in the same mood when you think about that fact over and over again, you become blind to the fact that you are analyzing that fact in the worst way.

Pay attention to your mood when you think of certain things and situations. For example, when you're feeling lonely and you think about your ex-girlfriend and how she lied to you, cheated on you, took money from you, what kind of facts do you think you will draw? What do you focus on? What kind of facts do you think you will become blind to?

Do you see how this works? Pay attention to your mood. Your mood might actually be putting you in a situation where you will constantly draw the wrong conclusions.

Now, let's flip the script. Let's say you're in a happy mood because you met somebody new. She's so awesome compared to all the women you've been with. Do you think about your ex-girlfriend at that point?

Probably not. You're in a good mood. You feel like you're on top of the world. Do you see how this works?

Do not neglect the importance of mood. It actually plays a bigger role than you think.

CHAPTER 6:

CBT BEST PRACTICES

Please take note of the following best practices. If you are seriously considering going through cognitive behavioral therapy, make sure that the therapist you're working with has the following best practices in place. If not, ask them if you can do the following. Whatever the case may be these best practices can help you get better results from your CBT therapy sessions. These therapy sessions do not have to involve face to face therapists.

You can do it online. You can go through some sort of assisted program. Whatever the case may be, there has to be an expert at the other side of the equation. You can't do this alone. That person must have the proper experience to guide you through the process so you can get optimal results.

Now, keep in mind that this is not a race. You're not trying to get from point A to point B as quickly as possible. The only person that is setting the pace of your progress is yourself. Take your time. You're trying to rebuild your life. Your life is built on your thoughts. You are your thoughts. And just as you can choose your thoughts, you can choose your life.

There's an old quote attributed to the ancient Chinese philosopher Confucius. It goes something like this, "If you sow a thought, you reap a word. When you sow a word, you reap an action. When you sow an action, you reap a habit. When you sow a habit, you reap a character. When you sow a character, you reap a destiny."

There's a lot of truth to this saying. Ultimately, you choose your destiny. How? On the surface, it's kind of mind-blowing because a destiny is huge, it's big, it takes forever. It's a work of a lifetime. It also has far-reaching impact.

Well, it all begins with the thoughts that you choose on a moment to moment basis. Just as a mighty river starts out as a tiny stream. Your destiny, as vast as it may be starts with a single thought. Those tiny streams that make up the White Nile flow together until it forms the Nile River. The same can be said about the Amazon River in Brazil.

It all has to start somewhere. Believe it or not, it starts out small. If you're not paying attention, you might not even notice. But if you take ownership of your thoughts and you actively choose them with the full understanding that they lead to somewhere big, and you choose your ultimate destination based on something big, you then put yourself in a situation where you are choosing your ultimate destination by choosing your thoughts in the here and now. The following best practices help you to do this.

DOCUMENT EVERYTHING

You should keep a journal that tracks your cognitive behavioral therapy progress. It doesn't have to be anything fancy. It doesn't have to have all sorts of graphs and charts. It doesn't have to have any of that. Instead, it can be just a simple diary. What is important is the date and the thoughts that you log. Even if you only have time for a few sentences, that's okay. As long as you are clear regarding your thoughts and your perceptions of those thoughts.

That's all you need to do because when you sit down with your therapist, you go through this material and you see your progression. You also able to pinpoint the impact of your mood or anything else that may be happening in your life and how it is reflected and how you judge your thoughts.

You should also track how your thoughts lead to action. What kind of actions do you normally take? Are you happy with those actions? Are there alternative paths you could have taken? Where do these lead back to? What kind of thoughts can these be traced back to? This journal is not only a diary but it is also a passport to a new life.

EXPOSE YOURSELF TO CHALLENGES

One of the most common reasons people undergo CBT involves phobias. They're afraid of going out into an open space where there are a lot of other people. They're afraid of meeting new people. They're afraid of spiders. They're afraid of heights, and so on and so forth. For CBT to work, you have to put pressure on your cognitive behavioral muscles. This means that you are going to make yourself uncomfortable. You can't just stand one thousand feet away from whatever it is that is stressing you out or causing all sorts of anxiety and depression and try to make changes. It doesn't work that way. This is just an intellectual exercise. You're just wasting your time if that's your attitude.

You have to get in the middle of things. You have to jump in. You have to feel it. You have to feel uncomfortable. You have to step out of your comfort zone. Now, this doesn't mean that you're going to put yourself in harm's way, don't overdo it. What this does mean, is that you have to allow yourself to be transformed by actual real-life experiences.

These gives you opportunities to carry-out the information that I have taught you so far. Without this valuable practice, you're just wasting your time. You might as well go to graduate school where you read case studies. Those case studies are actual businesses. They actually make or lose money. They have real flesh and blood human employees. Those are case studies, they're real. But you're dealing with them in an unreal way. You're dealing with them in a cold antiseptic secure place. You're dealing with them in an intellectual way. Well, if you want this stuff that you've read in this book, to truly help you change your life and turn things around, you have to put them into action.

You have to expose yourself to things that you fear. You have to intentionally put yourself into situation where you may become uncomfortable. And that's perfectly okay because it feels so much better when you overcome your fear. That's where you gain a sense of accomplishment. You've done something big. You have overcome.

AVOID FAKE SUBSTITUTES

There are sorts of fake substitutes to the mental and emotional heavy lifting you should be doing to get out from under your unhealthy personal assumptions. This can take many forms. Maybe you go to fortune tellers, maybe you watch a lot of YouTube videos of people doing all sorts of mentalist tricks. Those are not going to help you. They really not. Palm readers can tell you what you want to hear but all they are doing is giving you a false sense of hope. The hope here is that somehow, someway have some sort of control over your future.

Well, the only way to do that is to get out from under the negative assumptions you have about your past which push you to make all sorts of negative interpretations in the here and now. These have a real effect because you take the wrong actions again and again and again. When you try to gain some sense of control about the future by talking to a fortune teller or reading horoscopes you're just numbing yourself. That's all you're doing. That's like taking drugs instead of dealing with depression.

That's like drinking a lot of coffee when you should be working on the project. You're just drinking coffee and reading. That's not helping you. You have to drink coffee and work. Stay away from false substitutes, as I said this can take many different forms. It can also take the form of your family, believe it or not.

If you know that you have to make serious career changes and you have to work on turning your income-generating abilities around, one common tactic people take is to just shift almost all their time to their family. On the surface this is awesome. I mean this is crucial because, at the end of the day, your loved ones must take priority. But the problem is you're overdoing it. You're using it as a form of escape.

Believe it or not, you're not doing them any favors because they are relying on you. You may not end up giving them the life that they deserve because you're afraid to confront your fears. For whatever reason, you don't want to step out of the shadow of your past and you always holds you back and drags you down from living up to your fullest potential. Who do you think suffers?

Obviously, it going to be you but it's also were to be people who depend on you. Do not use your family as a crutch. That's the worst thing you can do to them. They're relying on you. They want you to be the best version of you. Unfortunately, the only person that can do that is you.

USE WORKAROUNDS TO SPEEDUP CBT'S EFFECTS

There are certain simple tricks that you can use to speed up the effects of the CBT. You can prepare yourself by asking yourself some stock questions. Whenever you feel triggered by let's say a negative memory, ask yourself, "Am I assuming too much? Is this the only interpretation? Am I seeing all the facts here? What am I basing this on? I know that this leads to something bad. Am I basing this on reality? Are there alternative conclusions to this?"

Come up with your own question. Come up with the question that really cuts you to the heart. Everybody's different so we tend to phrase our questions differently so it's okay. But come up with your own version that grabs your attention. You want to come up with a series of questions that stops you on your tracks when you otherwise could be riding that emotional rollercoaster and there is no stopping it.

You get triggered, you start assuming all the worst things and then you feel really bad and then you end up making a decision that you regret later on. This happens again and again and again, becomes a habit. You feel that this is just part of you. There's nothing you can do to change it. That's not true, that's a lie. Wake up to the lie.

Do yourself a big favor, come up with packed questions. These are canned questions that you always come back to so you can arrest, freeze, stop or thwart that rollercoaster that starts with your thoughts.

As I mentioned in a previous chapter, the world is essentially neutral. It's sending you all sorts of neutral signals. It's up to you to make the interpretation. It's the interpretation that counts more than the stimuli. Your interpretation can make your life heaven or hell. Guess what? It all turns on your ability to respond. Take ownership of that. Don't feel that you're just watching this movie that's going to play out regardless of what you do or regardless of how you feel.

That's a powerless way of looking at your life. And you look at that movie, please understand that you write the script. You direct the cameras. You edit whatever shows up on the screen. And most importantly, you act in it. You play all the roles believe it or not. Take ownership of this process by having a ready-list of questions that stop the flow or the speed at which you make interpretations. Get out from under generalization, assumptions or irrelevant thoughts that have always held you back.

STOP BLAMING OTHERS

What if I told you that the moment you blame other people you are handing them control over your life. Now, you might be thinking this is illogical. After all, these people actually caused you harm. They actually did something negative to you. Now you're going to ask me not to blame them? Well, think of it this way. While it's true that these people are the actual practical and logical cause of what happened to you, how you respond to that fact can hold you back and keep you down. It can prevent you from living a life full of possibility and power.

How? Well, you keep blaming them. Sure, they actually caused the problem but your response is not optimal. It doesn't lead to a sense of possibility. It doesn't lead to a sense of power. Why? Simple logic, if somebody is to blame for whatever happened to you, then they also have the solution, the fix. They can fix it because they caused it. This is how your internal logic works. You may not be aware of it but it's there.

Accordingly, you don't have to change. This is the big reward the people really are shooting for when they blame. These two are interlinked by assigning the blame to somebody else or situation beyond your control, you also give them the power to change things. This also has a matching effect on you because it freezes you from the responsibility of having to lift a finger to change your situation.

Sure you got abused in the past, sure you got cheated, embarrassed, humiliated, degraded, you name it. Those happen. Those people are logically to blame. Now what? So what? You'll have to live your life here and now. Those people have moved on. That ex-girlfriend that cheated on you and took your money, she has a family now. She's a Born-again Christian, she's happy, she's moved on. But you're still miserable. That boss that you felt degraded you in that meeting has become a billionaire. He's moved on.

But my question to you is, are you ready to move on or you going to continue to give them the power to change your life? Because that's what you're really doing. You're equating the logical cause of whatever hurt you in the here and now with the ability to turn things around. Well, you need to split that up. You really do. Yes, those people in those situations are to blame. Yes, you had a bad childhood. Yes, your father left you when you're two years old, abandoned you. Yes, your Mama abused you.

It doesn't matter. Those are in the past. They did cause those things. But the responsibility for your life lies squarely with you. Take ownership of that responsibility. You can't get those people to come back and fix your life, that's just not going to happen. You can't jump into some sort of time machine to go back and reverse what happened. You have to change how you respond now because when you do that you claim the power of turning your life around.

You also reject the cheap reward that you get of irresponsibility. This doesn't get you off the hook. Get used to it. Is it unfair? Absolutely! Does it suck? You're right. But it's your responsibility. Take ownership right here, right now. Stop blaming. It's not going to do anybody one bit of good.

STOP PERSONALIZING

One of the most common issues people are confronted with is when they look at situations that happen in the past and they personalize them. For example, they made a mistake but they personalize this as "The Loser." So they put their name, let's say your name is Joe Blow, the Loser. If you find yourself doing this, stop personalizing. That is not Joe Blow. Your past does not define you. So you cheated, you lied, you screwed around on your girlfriend or boyfriend but that doesn't have to define you. That was you in a given time and in a given place. Forgive yourself. Let go of that because you're more than that.

Believe it or not, there are lots of beautiful, good, kind and loving people in this world who have done really horrible stuff. They have abused kids, they've abused drugs, they've stolen, they've lied, they've broken all sorts of laws, and they manipulated people.

SO WHAT? NOW WHAT?

Keep asking those two questions because when you ask them in this context you quickly realize that your past does not have to define you. Your crimes are not the only source of your identity. Your sins do not make up your complete moral DNA as a person. You see where I'm coming from? Good. Take ownership of this. Understand that who you are is a choice and it's a choice made moment by moment.

It all boils down to the thoughts you choose. It all boils down to your analysis of what you have perceiving because if you want a better destiny for yourself then pay attention to how your choices of thoughts lead to that destiny. You may have come from a family of drug addicts, sex addicts, prostitutes, pimps, criminals, it doesn't matter. You are in control of your life.

Do not let anybody fool you into thinking you don't have that control. This is basic responsibility and self-ownership. Step up.

Unfortunately, when you personalize past failures and say, "Ah that's Joe Blow The Loser, that's me," you're dooming yourself. You're making yourself out some sort of flat two-dimensional cartoon. You're not just a series of actions. Maybe that was just you in the past. That was a particular point in time. Maybe you are hooked on heroin. So what? You can get off that habit. You can turn your life around. You can face your fear straight in the eye and overcome that fear and become a better person. And guess what happens, nobody has the right to dismiss you. Because if anything you are better than them.

They didn't have to overcome a childhood of abuse. They didn't have to overcome heroin addiction. They didn't have to overcome being a prostitute or being trafficked. You have to walk a mile in your shoes. Who are they to judge you? Please understand that the worst judge of your character that you will ever face is yourself. So judge right. Your past does not have to define you. Stop personalizing. Stop reducing yourself into a series of mistakes and bad judgments.

ADOPT MINDFULNESS

There are many mindfulness methods you can adopt so you can become more perceptive of your thoughts. Can be very formal. I am of course talking about meditation. Meditation is thousands of years old and there are many different "flavors" of meditation. Some are mystical and religious than others. A lot have a specific spirituality that they are closely associated with. Others are more stripped down. They're focused more on how your mind works.

Whatever the case may be, pick a form of mindfulness that you can stick to consistently. It can be something as basic as breathing deeply and then stopping for five seconds and then breathing out and then stopping for five seconds and then repeating this process until you're fully relaxed. You can also try present sense mindfulness where you basically just look at something in front of you. Right now, I'm looking at a fan. So I'd look straight at the middle of the fan and focus all my perception on it.

Eventually, I'm not seeing anything else and just seeing the fan and its' background. I freeze my thoughts. This is the essence of mindfulness because mindfulness really is all about training yourself to focus on the present moment. In any given second you're thinking about all sorts of stuff. You're thinking about the rent that has to be paid, you're thinking about driving your kids to soccer practice, you're thinking about ordering a latte from Starbucks, you're thinking about a million things.

When you practice mindfulness you unclench. It's as if you went from carrying many different shopping bags to dropping everything and just focusing on that one small envelope in front of you. It doesn't matter how you do it. You can count your breath, you can acknowledge your thoughts, you can use a mantra, and you can practice visualization. There are a million and one ways to get to the same place. What's important is that you get there. Because this ability enables you to focus on the truth of your thoughts which lead you to become a better analysis of your personal reality.

With this skillset, you become a more relaxed person. You're able to divorce your emotions from your thoughts. Just because certain things are happening around you doesn't mean that you have to react in the worst way possible. You may have done that in the past but that doesn't mean that you have to do it now.

Keep these best practices in mind because they go a long way in helping you get out from under the negative interpretations that are making you suffer. You have to understand and remember that these are interpretations. You're the one making the interpretation. You are always in control. Take full ownership and responsibility of this ability and you will start living a better life. There's nobody else to blame except yourself. There is no better time than now. Do it. You owe it to yourself and your loved ones.

CONCLUSION

Cognitive behavioral therapy has helped countless people through the years overcome fears, anxieties, and negative mental habits that kept them from living a happier, more fulfilling life. CBT can help you too... if you let it.

The information you read in this book is not self-executing. You can't just read this book and all of a sudden, your life starts to improve. CBT doesn't work that way.

Oftentimes, recovery can be an uncomfortable if not painful process. How come? We have to overcome our mental habits. We have to purposefully change the way we look at life, ourselves, and how we view our personal capabilities. This means overcoming fear, dealing with pride, and committing to confronting our personal issues right in the eyes...

The good news? The more you practice CBT-regardless of how low level your starting point may be-the better you'll get at it. You'll grow in confidence and you'll be able to achieve better and better results. It all boils down to choosing to start right now. Right here.

I wish you nothing but the best in your quest for a happier, more fulfilling, more meaningful life.

Cognitive Behavioral Therapy

Master Your Brain and Emotions to Overcome Anxiety, Depression, and Negative Thoughts

By BILL ANDREWS

http://geni.us/cbtbook

INTRODUCTION

THIS IS MY STORY

I've always been shy. I'm not just talking about the kind of garden-variety shyness most people occasionally suffer from. My shyness, to quote the legendary 80s band The Smiths' song "How Soon Is Now," was "criminally vulgar."

I would freeze up – as in physically freeze up. In many cases, I would get scared stiff of having to speak to a crowd of strangers or even meet new people in an unfamiliar place. I didn't want to leave home. That's how bad it was for me.

In fact, every time I had to meet someone new, make a presentation, or otherwise have to be physically in front of people I didn't already know, I would get close to becoming physically sick. Even if I didn't throw up, the physical effects of my shyness really frustrated me. I would get cold sweats. I would feel light headed.

In some cases, I would feel temporarily "deaf." People would talk to me, but I could barely hear what they're saying. In many cases, there were "dead spots" in the words that I was hearing from them. I would try to pass it off by smiling or nodding my head.

Not surprisingly, all these "issues" crippled my social life. And that's only the physical effects of my shyness – the emotional and psychological self-torture that I endured were brutal as well.

Indeed, things got so bad that I thought I would never find anyone to share my life with. My work prospects were very limited since almost all jobs require some sort of interpersonal or public contact. I was at the end of my rope.

I thought I was a hopeless basket case – an irredeemable victim of my own personal neuroses – until I went on a trip with friends to Italy. In between sights at ancient Roman ruins, my best friend told me that my issues were all in my head. He sat me down and broke everything down for me:

- I had a great degree from a top, world-class university.
- I had a great job and a great income – an income most people would love to have.
- I had no debt.
- Everything I possessed, I owned outright.
- I did not have any student debt.
- I was in shape.
- I was not a bad-looking guy.

On and on he went. He was forcing me to look at my life and the stories I chose to believe about myself from a totally different perspective. He was pushing me to look at myself from a perspective I don't usually use. Indeed, most of the time, I was completely unaware of the things I had going for me.

That's when everything changed. My buddy Raul chipped away at the "mental cocoon" I had built for myself. For the longest time, my comfort zone's walls provided me with some measure of comfort. Little did I know, the more I retreated into my fear of people (and rejection), the more the walls of my comfort zone caved in around me. It became my personal mental prison.

After that trip, as I was drinking coffee alone at the company dining hall, I asked myself a very simple question. It turned out to be the key to me turning my life around. I asked myself, "Is this all my life has to offer?" I was staring at the bottom of my empty coffee cup. I could see the droplets of coffee slowly swirling around the coffee cup as I moved it. I kept asking myself that question as I stared at the nearly-empty bottom of my cup. At that point, I made a decision. I made it my personal mission to punch, kick, shoot through, or bulldoze the walls of my personal comfort zone.

Now, I'm able to make presentations to business groups anywhere from Tokyo to Toronto. I'm able to strike up conversations with strangers anywhere – from train stations to airplanes to packed bars. Best of all, I'm able to set them (and myself) at ease.

I also met the love of my life. It took me taking courage and boldly marching out of my comfort zone (and personal shell) for me to meet her... finally!

I was able to do all these because of the one key revelation and personal realization that shot through my brain like a thousand crystal bullets that summer in Rome so many years ago.... I realized I have a tremendous amount of CONTROL over what I choose to FEEL, DO and DEFINE MYSELF AS. In other words, by simply taking ownership of what I choose to believe about myself, I can change my life.

A few years later, I found out that there was actually a scientific name for this personal revelation of mine: **cognitive behavioral therapy or CBT**.

In this book, I'm going to share with you some practical CBT techniques that can help you overcome fear, limitations, depression, anxiety, emotional over reaction, extreme emotional sensitivity, and other negative states of mind.

Take note: I have consciously written this book in plain English as much as possible. As powerful as the concepts and exercises CBT may bring to the table may be, a lot (too much!) of the professional literature out there seems to be written for psychologists by psychologists, psychiatrists, and other mental health professionals. It seems that they are just speaking to themselves and a lot is lost in translation.

I have taken a different tack. I've written this book using very accessible terms so you can get a clear and actionable set of practices. Apply these to whatever personal issues you're grappling with. That's right. You don't have to have a master's degree or a PhD to understand, put into use, and benefit from the key CBT information contained in this book.

WHO IS THIS BOOK FOR?

This book is for people who are having a tough time dealing with low self-esteem, low self-confidence, social fears, depression, or who constantly think negative and limiting thoughts.

The bottom line? By changing your thought patterns and assumptions, you can make positive changes in your life. These changes help you become a happier, more content person capable of living life with a full sense of well-being and contentment.

GET THIS BOOK HERE

http://geni.us/cbtbook

END OF PREVIEW

****

FREE Mini E-Book

Thank you for reading this book. As a way of showing my appreciation, I want to give you a **FREE Mini E-Book** along with this book.

This FREE book will take you to the path of **Ultimate Life Success**.

What You'll Get Inside?

3 Powerful Techniques To Power Up Your Mind In The Direction Of Wealth, Happiness & Success!!

PLEASE VISIT BELOW URL TO DOWNLOAD

http://geni.us/freecbt

****

TO READ MORE BOOKS BY BILL ANDREWS, PLEASE VISIT

http://geni.us/billbooks

Made in the USA
Columbia, SC
01 December 2018